P9-DNK-263

as is

The Role of Mind in Hugo,
Faulkner, Beckett, and
Grass

# The Role of Mind in Hugo, Faulkner, Beckett, and Grass

MARTHA O'NAN

PHILOSOPHICAL LIBRARY
New York

Copyright, 1969, by PHILOSOPHICAL LIBRARY, INC.
15 East 40 Street, New York, N. Y. 10016
*All rights reserved*

Library of Congress Catalog Card No. 78-86505

MANUFACTURED IN THE UNITED STATES OF AMERICA

# CONTENTS

## ACKNOWLEDGMENTS

I wish to thank members of the Ohio University Research Committee for a grant which was used to prepare part of this book.

I am particularly indebted to Dr. Mary E. Knapp for a wide range of scholarly advice and generosity.

MARTHA O'NAN

State University of New York
Brockport, New York

# CHAPTER I

# Introduction

> Thus "mind" and "mental" are
> merely approximate concepts,
> giving a convenient shorthand
> for certain approximate laws.
>
> —*Bertrand Russell*

The mind plays an important role in the lives of Victor Hugo's Quasimodo, William Faulkner's Benjy, Samuel Beckett's Lucky, and Günter Grass's Oskar. Theories of mind which pertain to Quasimodo are found in the works of Locke, the eighteenth-century French *philosophes*, and Maine de Biran; a theory for Benjy is found in the writings of Briquet, Janet, and Freud; Lucky can be explained by "history" and especially in terms of Bergson's philosophy; and Oskar seems to belong in both essentialist and existentialist worlds.

So much light was thrown upon the mind by Locke's sensationalism that the eighteenth-century philosopher, Helvétius, concluded: "By Locke, old man was destroyed and there was born a new man who marches toward truth."[1] A "new man" would emerge, it was believed, from the discovery that the mind depends upon sensations. The formula was: many sensations, many ideas; no sensations, no ideas.[2]

Unable to accept the mind as being completely the product of external sensations, Maine de Biran stated in 1803

1

that the mind was also directed by inner forces such as instinct, will, passions, and conscience.[3] His work was summarized by Henri Bergson: "Quite contrary to Kant . . . Maine de Biran concluded that the human mind was capable, at least to a degree, of reaching the absolute and making it the object of speculation."[4]

Coming to the mind itself, Bergson and Freud conceived of exploring it through the unconscious. The inner nature of the mind was held by Freud to be the unconscious which he described in 1900 as being "the true psychic reality; *in its inner nature it is just as much unknown to us as the reality of the external world, and it is just as imperfectly communicated to us by the data of consciousness as is the external world by the reports of our sense-organs.*"[5]

In 1901, Bergson spoke of the unconscious as the subject of future psychology: "To explore the unconscious, to work in the subsoil of the mind with highly specialized methods will be the principal task of psychology in the century which is beginning. I have little doubt but that there will be discoveries perhaps as important as those in the physical and natural sciences of the past centuries."[6] Bergson thought, too, of the mind as being subject to stagnation in the "mechanical."

On every side, there has always been uncertainty as to the exact nature of the mind. Centuries ago, Lucretius wrote in *De Rerum natura* that the "darkness of the mind must be dispelled. . . ." But the same darkness caused Ionesco to be repetitious when he admitted in 1960 that "the space inside ourselves is immense. Who dares venture there? We need explorers, discoverers of unknown worlds which are in us, which are yet to be discovered in us."[7]

In the rise and fall of theories of mind, many fictional characters have had roles. Significant among these are Quasimodo in *Notre-Dame de Paris* (1831), Benjy in *The Sound and the Fury* (1929), Lucky in *Waiting for Godot* (1952), and Oskar in *The Tin Drum* (1959).

2

# CHAPTER II

# Victor Hugo's Quasimodo: the Senses

> . . . ugly like an evildoer.
>
> —*Gabriela Mistral*

The mind makes it possible for only Quasimodo to play the role of Quasimodo. He is not Spenser's savage man who "liv'd all on ravin and rape," or Shakespeare's deformed Caliban "got by the devil," or one of Montaigne's cannibals, or Voltaire's polished Huron, or J.-J. Rousseau's happy primitive man. Quasimodo is a unique "natural" man who lived in fifteenth-century Paris and yet had a mind formed according to certain principles of sensationalism set forth by John Locke in the seventeenth century in *An Essay Concerning Human Understanding.*

Quasimodo made his first appearance in *Notre-Dame de Paris,* silently but dreadfully on January 6, 1482, the Feast of the Kings and the Festival of the Fools. Having by far the most monstrous grimace in the contest for the selection of the pope of the fools, he won and, afterwards, displayed before the mob his "little left eye obstructed by a bushy, red eyebrow" and his right eye "completely hidden under an enormous wart."[1]

The mob strained for a better view of his "huge head with stiff, red hair; his enormous hump with a rebound in his chest" (p. 37). Banded together, the mob became fearless and even mocked the hunchback, while normally one or even several men would flee from his eye staring at them, sometimes from a dark street and sometimes from the shad-

3

ows of the cathedral where in his presence mouths and eyes opened and dogs howled.

His many deformities caused the public to call him a beast, a vile monkey, something which should have been thrown into water or fire. His hideous face, it was thought, could frighten a woman into abortion. It was said that he could fly like a witch and that his eye, covered by a wart, was "an egg containing another similar devil, which had another little egg containing another devil, and so on" (p. 113). He could also "turn men into stone which he took to build towers. He commanded fifty legions" (p. 355).

Yet, all these ugly features do not completely explain why he was so feared. What really terrified the people of Paris was what was on his mind. Even though they had never heard him "speak his mind," they were certain that his thoughts were evil. They would have accepted as an accurate self-portrait (had he talked) the confession made by Hugo's monster, Han d'Islande, that he liked most of all to have "living human flesh quiver under his teeth and smoking blood warm his thirsty palate."[2] Quasimodo's mind was read by unthinking prejudice and, therefore, incorrectly. His mind was not made in the image of his ugly, deformed body, but the people of Paris could never have imagined that.

However, the question of how his character's mind functioned was raised by Hugo who did not conclude hastily that an ugly body is matched by an ugly mind. Before publishing *Notre-Dame de Paris,* Hugo had discussed the ugly and the beautiful in the *Préface* of *Cromwell* (1828) and had explained that "everything in creation is not humanly *beautiful,* that the ugly exists side by side with the beautiful, the deformed near the graceful. . . ."[3] Continuing to be fascinated by the ugly, he wrote in the introduction to *Littérature et philosophie mêlées* that it was the duty of the writer "to show, whenever the occasion presented itself, a beautiful personality under physical deformity."[4] The dic-

4

tum pronounced by Hugo is not that a beautiful personality in a deformed body is more ideal than a beautiful personality in a beautiful body. It is simply that the true rather than the ideal places the ugly with the beautiful and the grotesque with the sublime, and one of these "true" characters is Quasimodo, a human gargoyle created to live in fifteenth-century Paris and given a mind from the pages of John Locke's seventeenth-century *Essay Concerning Human Understanding*.

Hugo's use of Locke is not at all surprising, for Locke's work—*L'Essai sur l'entendement humain de Locke*—was on the university list of books prepared in 1809 in France for students in philosophy.[5] In 1816, Hugo was a student in philosophy and mathematics at the Collège Royal de Louis Le Grand, and the first philosophical term in his notebook was "sensation," one of the most important words in Locke's *Essay*.[6] Hugo also defined Locke's philosophy, as he understood it, in the "Journal d'un jeune jacobite de 1819" by a concise question and answer: " 'What does exist mean?' asked Locke. 'To feel.' "[7] This definition can be applied to Quasimodo whose system of senses was in such bad repair that his sensations, Hugo imagined, became lost in blind alleys and on dead-end streets.

Psychologically, Quasimodo is a subject whose development is retarded by poor sight and, later, by the additional handicap of deafness. In his successive loss of senses, his experience is opposite that of the statue which Condillac in the eighteenth century "awakened" by the smell of a rose into a world where the marble learned through sensations to become self-conscious.[8] Unlike the statue, Quasimodo was born with all senses. He had an impairment in sight and was to suffer the loss of hearing when he was fourteen years old.

With his decreasing senses, he illustrates the psychology of sensations which in the early nineteenth century was explained by Maine de Biran in *Influence de l'habitude sur*

5

*la faculté de penser* (1803), a work presenting the theory that "the production of ideas is no more than the result or consequence of the activity of the impressions themselves."[9] Maine de Biran's theory was in the tradition of Locke as were those theories held about sensations in the eighteenth century by La Mettrie, Helvétius, Condillac, and Diderot. But he emphasized more than they did the belief that "one vainly would look on the outside" for all the causes of will, passions, and conscience.[10] As for the influence of the eighteenth century, it has been pointed out by J.-B. Barrère that the effect of Hugo's extensive reading of eighteenth-century writers has received too little scholarly attention.[11]

This omission may have been encouraged by Hugo himself who often made statements against that century: ". . . philosophy of the eighteenth century . . . is no less hostile toward poetry than religion, because poetry like religion is no more than a great synthesis. Voltaire committed heresy no less against Homer than Jesus."[12] Yet, Hugo's hostility indicates awareness of the eighteenth century. Whenever the influence of the eighteenth century upon Hugo is considered in detail, Locke's contribution to that century cannot be neglected. But an even more direct reason for including Locke is Hugo's own mention of him.

Writing about the senses in *An Essay Concerning Human Understanding*, Locke made many statements which may be used to describe the fictional character, Quasimodo. A particularly applicable quotation from Locke is one dealing with those ideas which can enter the mind through only one sense and for which there is no substitute door or postern; these senses do not have back doors or gates or, as in fortifications, false doors; there are only front doors:

> There are some ideas which have admittance only through one sense, which is particularly adapted to receive them. Thus light and colours, as white, red, yellow, blue, with their several degrees or shades and

mixtures, as green, scarlet, purple, sea-green, and the rest, come in only by the eyes; all kinds of noises, sounds, and tones only by the ears; the several tastes and smells, by the nose and palate. And if these organs, or the nerves, which are the conduits to convey them from without to their audience in the brain—the mind's presence-room, as I may so call it—are any of them so disordered as not to perform their functions, they have no postern to be admitted by, no other way to bring themselves into view, and be perceived by the understanding.[13]

The French translation of Locke's *Essay,* made in 1700 by Pierre Coste and republished in Hugo's time, follows the English closely as the following sentence illustrates:

Et si les organes ou nerfs, qui après avoir reçu ces impressions de dehors, les portent au cerveau, qui est, pour ainsi-dire, la chambre d'audience, où elles se présentent à l'âme, pour y produire différentes sensations; si, dis-je, quelques-uns de ces organes viennent à être détraqués, ensorte qu'ils ne puissent point éxercer leur fonction, ces sensations ne sçauroient y être admises par quelque fausse porte: elles ne peuvent plus se présenter à l'entendement, et en être apperçuës par aucune autre voye.[14]

"Organs," "nerves," "mind's presence-room," and "postern" are kept in the translation made by Coste who stated in the edition of 1700 that he had consulted Locke about certain difficulties in translation: ". . . if I have ever taken any liberty (for that cannot be avoided), it has always satisfied Mr. Locke who understood French well enough to judge when I was translating correctly his thought."[15] Among later editions of Coste's translation of *Essai philosophique concernant l'entendement humain* were those of 1742 and

1750. Within Hugo's life time, Coste's translations of Locke's works were brought together in seven volumes of *Oeuvres philosophiques de Locke,* trans. Coste (Paris: F. Didot, 1821-1825).

Locke used the term, "postern," in the meaning of substitute sense organ, and the eighteenth-century *philosophes,* such as Diderot, used the word, *"porte,"* for the sense organ itself. For example, Diderot wrote that "les connaissances ont trois portes pour entrer dans notre âme. . . ."[16] Hugo, too, used the word, *"porte,"* when writing about Quasimodo's failing senses: "La seule porte que la nature lui eût laissée toute grande ouverte sur le monde s'était brusquement fermée à jamais" (p. 120).

The first *"porte,"* "door," belonging to Quasimodo which fails to open into his "mind's presence-room" is one of his eyes. The misfortune of having only one functioning eye was naturally observed by curious women the Sunday after Easter when he was left in a sack at the place for foundlings in the cathedral.[17] The little monster, who the good ladies said should have had a vampire for a wet nurse, shed tears that day from his one eye and predicted unhappy things to come in his enactment of a short tragedy of doom.

As Quasimodo grew older, his eye became the butt of jokes which on one occasion were interrupted by an educated but dissipated young man, Jehan Frollo, who wisely said that "a one-eyed person is more incomplete than a blind person" (p. 39). The one-eyed person knows what he lacks. The fact may be true, but there is a misapplication based upon the assumption that Quasimodo at one time had had sight in both eyes and that having lost sight in one eye understood his loss. It is plain that, never having had two functioning eyes, Quasimodo could never have understood fully his handicap.

The commentator, Jehan Frollo, was an actual person in the fifteenth century[18] and, therefore, could not be expected to understand perfectly seventeenth-century sensationalist theories. Even earlier in *Notre-Dame de Paris*, he had been associated with centuries yet to come when his shrill cry was described as exceeding the limit of perceptible sounds, "twelve thousand vibrations according to Sauveur or eight thousand according to Biot" (pp. 35-36). Jehan lived two hundred years before Joseph Sauveur (1653-1716) who, though deaf, made important contributions to music and the science of sounds and acoustics.[19] And Jehan lived three hundred years before Jean-Baptiste Biot (1774-1862), a physicist and mathematician whose work, being on the university list of books prepared in 1809 for students in mathematics, was possibly read by Hugo in student days.[20]

Jehan spanned centuries. When he let himself be a man of the Middle Ages and especially when he was himself, his psychological analysis of Quasimodo was, it might be said, that he was deaf and therefore absurd or *"surdus absurdus,"* a quotation from Jean-Amos Coménius (1592-1671), used by Hugo to explain the laughter of the crowd enjoying the "farce" of Quasimodo being beaten on the wheel (p. 189).[21]

But Hugo did not think of Quasimodo as being absurd. In a letter dated December 5, 1833, and written to Mademoiselle Louise Bertin, he explained that he was enclosing Quasimodo's song which he had made as gay as possible for her opera, *La Esmeralda,* but that it was impossible for the song to be foolishly gay or *"folâtre."*[22] Even though a deaf, comic, *"folâtre"* Quasimodo would have been quite authentic for the Middle Ages and even for Hugo's Middle Ages, Hugo preferred another type of Quasimodo for his novel: a one-eyed, deaf Quasimodo who, had he lived in later centuries, might have been "scientifically" interesting to Locke and the *philosophes.* However, the table of time was reversed, and it was Jehan Frollo of the fifteenth century who revealed some knowledge of theories of sensationalism of the seventeenth, eighteenth, and nineteenth centuries. Jehan was

9

beyond his time when he said that "a one-eyed person is more incomplete than a blind person," because the one-eyed person knows what he lacks. However, like most generalizations, Jehan's generalization does not apply to the situation—that is, to Quasimodo who had lost no part of his sense of sight. He had always been one-eyed.

However, a sense which Quasimodo did lose was hearing: "The only door which nature had left opening wide onto the world had been suddenly closed forever" (p. 120). Being fourteen years old, he was sufficiently mature to know what he was to lack. The circumstances for his new affliction were provided by his profession, bell-ringer of the cathedral. More than bell-ringer. A permanent inhabitant of the old church, for he lived and slept there until he had almost taken its form, "just as a snail takes the form of its shell" (p. 119). Even here, the cruelest fate was active in the life of the foundling who encountered in his work huge bells with vibrations strong enough to split the tympanic membranes of his ears.

Upon learning that Quasimodo was deaf, Robin Poussepain asked whether he could talk: "[Quasimodo] looks at you; he is one-eyed. You speak to him; he is deaf. What in the devil does that Polyphemus do with his tongue?" (p. 39). Quasimodo is not Polyphemus, the Cyclops blinded by Ulysses. But the question about his tongue is valid: does deafness cause a loss of speech? Commenting upon the relationship of speech and hearing, Maine de Biran wrote that "if we talk because we hear, it is true to say that we understand only as well as we talk; the two organs act and react upon each other without ceasing."[23] Thus it was natural for Quasimodo to cease talking after he had become deaf.

A significant exception to his usual silence occurred while he was keeping Esmeralda in the cathedral. His words at that time may be those discussed with Victor Hugo in 1843 by Professor Ferdinand Berthier of the Institution Nationale des Sourds-Muets in Paris.[24] However, even though

10

Quasimodo spoke to Esmeralda, he could not understand what she said and had to ask her to "speak" to him by means of signs and gestures. It would seem that deafness and muteness were separating him more and more from the external world in contrast to the Pygmalion-like awakening of Condillac's statue.

The effect of the diminution of senses was understood by Hugo in the terms of the psychology of sensation. "It is certain," he wrote in reference to Quasimodo, "that the mind becomes atrophied in an incomplete body. . . . The impressions which Quasimodo received from objects underwent a considerable refraction before reaching his thoughts" (p. 121). Furthermore, he suffered "a thousand optical illusions, a thousand errors in judgment, a thousand deviations where his thought wandered sometimes foolishly and sometimes idiotically" (p. 121).

The illusions are not supplied nor the errors enumerated by Hugo. Nevertheless, he imagined that Quasimodo's mental mechanism, severed from sensations, was withering away in impenetrable darkness. "If we were now to try to reach Quasimodo's soul across that thick and hard shell; if we were to sound the depths of that badly made body; if we could take a torch . . . to cast suddenly a bright light on the psyche enchained in the bottom of that cavern, we could doubtlessly find the poor wretch in some sort of pathetic, stunted, rickety attitude like those prisoners of the jails of Venice who grew old bent double in a stone cell much too low and short" (p. 121). This is Quasimodo whose mind was starved from the lack of sensations.

He remained incomplete because his imperfect senses of sight and hearing limited the number and accuracy of sensations coming into his "mind's presence-room." He could not fulfill completely Locke's definition of "exist" as set forth by Hugo: " 'What does exist mean?' asked Locke. 'To feel.' " When Hugo introduced the general concept of Locke's sensationalism into Quasimodo's life, he explained his character not by science of the Middle Ages but by science of later centuries. Perhaps to save himself from too much science or perhaps even to arrive at greater truth, Hugo excused the unknown of Quasimodo's mind by stating that in 1482 the "microscope had not yet been invented either for things of matter or for things of the mind" (p. 191).

# CHAPTER III

# William Faulkner's Benjy: Hysteria

"Evil and further evil,
and a curse cursed on our
children. . . ."

—*Ezra Pound*

Hysteria, reaching a level of frenzy and fear and sometimes ending in a convulsion, is found in Benjy and in various other Faulkner characters. The dogs in "The Bear" were often frantic and scared and had "voices high, abject, almost human in their hysteria."[1] Nancy of "That Evening Sun" was hysterical as she moaned "Jeeeeeeeeeeeeeeeesus, until the sound went out, like a match or candle does" (p. 535). She was so certain of being murdered some night by her husband, Jesus, that she had her "coffin money saved up" (p. 544). She attempted suicide in jail and possibly, like Quentin Compson, "loved death above all" (p. 242). But her end did not come until *Requiem for a Nun*.

The hysterical dogs and characters were suffering from fear which, Faulkner pointed out in his speech upon the award of the Nobel Prize for Literature, is catastrophic in human lives: "Our tragedy today is a general and universal physical fear so long sustained by now that we can even bear it" (p. 3). And he continued by saying that the young person "must teach himself that the basest of all things is to be afraid . . ." (p. 3).

13

The toll from fear and hysteria was heavy among the Compsons: Mrs. Compson was an invalid; Mr. Compson, an alcoholic; Jason, a sadist; Quentin, a suicide; and Benjy, a moaner. To diagnose their illness as being hysteria is impossible, because hysteria has not been described satisfactorily in medicine in spite of centuries of study beginning with ancient philosophers and physicians of the fame of Hippocrates, Celsus, Aretaeus, Galen, Aëtius, and Paul of Aegina. Modern physicians likewise have failed to define the word. The physician, René Cruchet, wrote in 1951 that hysteria is a "mental process which, let us admit, still all but completely escapes us."[2]

Observation continues to be the principal means of studying hysteria, and here Faulkner could offer the Compsons as cases for clinical study. In hysteria, Pierre Janet wrote, "One must distrust complicated experiments which are not easily made on the mind; the apparatus is enough to upset the mental state that one wishes to study. . . . One must, therefore, put the patient in simple, carefully planned situations and note exactly and at every moment what he will say and do. Examining actions and words is the best means of knowing men. . . . Words, writings of the patients are true documents . . . ; it goes without saying that one must interpret them."[3] Faulkner certainly observed hysterical tendencies and placed them in varying degrees in the Compsons. Their story—and especially the story of their victim, Caddy—is writen in Benjy's unconscious, filled by his omniscient senses for a period of some thirty years. But, first of all, Benjy told his own story.

His story is found in his moaning and playing "graveyard." Anyone who saw him on the day of his story, April 7, 1928, would have said that he was a big man, thirty-three years old, and an idiot who moaned and slobbered unless he was holding his "graveyard." No one would have imagined that this sad creature had memories. But, of course, he had. Therefore, memories must be added so that a description of his one day includes memories, moaning, and a graveyard.

Memories and hysteria were found existing together by Freud. There is, however, a question of associating Freud and Faulkner, for Faulkner said: "Freud, I'm not familiar with."[4] But this statement may not mean that Freud's observations should not be used in criticism, because Faulkner remarked: "I think—I'm convinced, though, that that sort of criticism whether it's nonsensical or not is valid because it is a symptom of change, of motion, which is life, and also it's proof that literature—art—is a living quantity in our social condition. If it were not, then, there'd be no reason for people to delve and find all sorts of symbolisms and psychological strains and currents in it."[5]

Perhaps the critic does delve into literature and does find all kinds of "symbolisms and psychological strains and currents in it." Certainly, Faulkner delved into life and came to some mystery in his idiot character, Benjy, who moaned and insisted on having a graveyard. Benjy is deep enough to merit the application of Freud's theory that *"hysterical patients suffer principally from reminiscences."*[6] Little can be said of Benjy's hysterical attack except that it was a day of anguished slobbering and moaning. During the day, Luster, in angry monosyllables, ordered Benjy: " 'Hush up that moaning' " (p. 5). " 'Shut up that moaning' " (p. 5). *"What are you moaning about . . ."* (p. 7). *"Can't you shut up that moaning and slobbering . . ."* (p. 9). *"Cry baby . . ."* (p. 12). " 'Now, git in that water and play and see can you stop that slobbering and moaning' " (p. 15). When some of Luster's acquaintances passed by, they said: " 'What does you do when he start bellering' " (p. 14). " 'What he moaning about now' " (p. 15). With little imagination as to the causes of the moaning, Luster answered: " 'Lawd knows. . . . He just starts like that' " (p. 15).

Yet from Luster came the information that Benjy did not moan every day. Luster described the length of the moaning: " 'He been at it all morning' " (p. 15). "All morning" designates one morning. Moreover, Luster thoughtlessly and ironically gave a reason for Benjy's hysterical behavior: " 'Cause it his birthday, I reckon' " (p. 15). Later, Luster complained: " 'He just trying hisself. . . . That the way he been going on all day' " (p. 51).

Since Benjy did not "beller" every day, there must have been an exact association which began the attack on Saturday, April 7. Here, Luster must bear the responsibility because he had taken Benjy to a place which awakened memories. Luster knew, like Dilsey, that the golf course and the branch were disturbing to Benjy, but when she asked Luster whether he had taken Benjy there, Luster with his devious blandness answered: " 'Nome. . . . We been right here in this yard all day, like 'you said' " (p. 46). But this was not true. Early in the morning, the two had been near the golf course and, then, on to the branch. Benjy started moaning as he watched the golfers and continued furiously at the branch.

The golf course and the branch should be placed in relation to Benjy's childhood, since the most important memories in hysteria are, according to Freud, those based upon the impressions of early experiences.[7] The branch is the scene of the earliest memory of Benjy who recalled having been there when he was three or four years old and still named "Maury." The golf course was built later when Benjy was about fifteen years old. From the golf course came a voice which called " 'here, caddie' " (p. 5), and suddenly Benjy's attack began. A mere word such as "caddie" (Caddy) is sufficient to begin an attack of hysteria which can last all day and can receive additional associative stimuli during the day. Pierre Janet described in 1910 a patient who was not unlike Benjy: "From time to time, several times a day, she thought about her unhappiness and let out a little groan. That beginning was enough; she could no longer stop and there she was letting out sharp, monotonous shouts which made her neighbors flee."[8]

After looking for the causes of hysteria, Freud concluded that *"a hysterical symptom originates only when two contrary wish-fulfillments having their source in different psychic systems are able to meet in a single expression."*[9] Benjy seems to meet these requirements. His two contrary wish-fulfillments are joy-sadness. His two psychic systems are the unconscious and the conscious. (It should be stressed, however, that he is almost all "unconscious." His bit of conscious is indicated by his moaning.) And his single expression is found in the jimson weeds in a bottle: his graveyard.

His earliest joyful-sad memories began the day his grandmother died. On that day, he was still named "Maury" and was at the branch with Caddy, his brothers, and Versh. Soon the children went home where they saw so many lights that they thought there was a party, but actually the occasion was the death of their grandmother. That night, the children were put to bed, all sleeping in one room: Jason with Quentin, and Caddy with Benjy ("Maury"). Dilsey did not have time to wash Caddy who at the branch had muddied her drawers: " 'Just look at you,' Dilsey said. She wadded the drawers and scrubbed Caddy behind with them. 'It done soaked clean through onto you,' she said. 'But you wont get no bath this night. Here' " (p. 58). All night long, Caddy smelled like trees in the rain just as she had "smelled like trees in the rain" (p. 17) while the children were at the branch. After that event, Benjy expressed joy when he "said" that Caddy smelled like trees or like trees in the rain. However, the emotion of sadness was also experienced by Benjy ("Maury") on the day his grandmother died when Caddy stressed the fact that "dogs are dead" and talked about buzzards eating Nancy (p. 27). Thus, his grandmother's death brought both sadness and joy, the two contrary emotions from which Benjy "invented" his pantomime of moaning and playing "graveyard."

17

Truthfully, it would be difficult to know whether he himself believed that his jimson weeds in a bottle made a graveyard. But such a question would lead to doubts about all the visions of color and motion which he had. For example, one night, the house lights shone through the sound and movement of the leaves onto the grass, and he probably expected flies to swarm from something dead as they had earlier in the day: "The trees were buzzing, and the grass" (p. 31). At another time, in an abandoned barn, he saw spider webs floating in the sun's rays: *"The slanting holes were full of spinning yellow"* (p. 12). This imaged language may well be the real reality of his mind. Equally real may be his pantomime of the graveyard.

The pantomime of hysteria was described by Freud: "When one psycho-analyzes a patient subject to hysterical attacks one soon gains the conviction that these attacks are nothing but phantasies projected and translated into motor activity and represented in pantomime."[10] Freud's pantomime seems to be similar to imitation and simulation found in hysteria by Pierre Briquet in 1859: ". . . that the various morbid phenomena which characterize hysteria are no more than the repetition of a certain number of vital acts by which the disturbances are revealed."[11] From these descriptions of hysterical attacks (fits or convulsions), it can be seen that Benjy's moaning and playing "graveyard" are a pantomime.

After the deaths of Quentin and Mr. Compson and the departure ("death") of Caddy, Benjy began to hold a "funeral" and moaned in his "graveyard," consisting of jimson weeds (flowers) in a bottle. Certainly he had "observed" that "folks" moan at funerals. He had even heard "funeral" defined on the day his grandmother had died as being an event "where they moans. . . . They moaned two days on Sis Beulah Clay" (p. 27). Moaning was an emotion of sadness for him.

But his graveyard was joy. Having learned that he cried

when his graveyard was taken away, Dilsey scolded her grandson, Luster, for that cruel act:

> "Aint you shamed of yourself." Dilsey said. "Teasing him." She set the cake on the table.
> "I aint been teasing him." Luster said. "He was playing with that bottle full of dogfennel and all of a sudden he started up bellering. You heard him."
> "You aint done nothing to his flowers." Dilsey said.
> "I aint touched his graveyard." Luster said. (pp. 44-45)

But as usual, Luster had been "projecking" with Benjy's graveyard which in Benjy's world was associated with joy and not mourning. Dilsey understood about the graveyard and the flowers. Once when Benjy and his mother were going to the cemetery to visit the graves of Mr. Compson and Quentin, she said: " 'Give him a flower to hold. . . . That what he wanting' " (p. 10).

It is strange indeed that a graveyard brought joy to Benjy. But the simple fact is that with funerals Caddy appeared: she took care of him and spent the night with him at the time of their grandmother's funeral; she came home for Quentin's funeral; and, against the family's wishes, she returned for Mr. Compson's funeral. Since Caddy attended funerals, Benjy used his graveyard for his immediate pleasure and perhaps even as a savage incantation to bring about another funeral which his sister might attend.

The emotions of joy and sadness have a long history in Benjy's life. While named "Maury," he experienced contrary emotions: joy with Caddy and sadness at the sight and smell of death. By some kind of cleverness, he developed his pantomime of the graveyard as a condensation of his joy and sadness. In face of the impossible, he attempted to keep unchanged the happiness which he associated with his sister. He developed an ironic, inadequate substitute for joy: a

19

graveyard. But the other Compsons knew better: they knew that the true use of graveyards was for burying themselves and others.

One of those "buried" was Caddy who, Mrs. Compson and Jason claimed, was a family disgrace. Part of her story is related by Benjy in his reminiscences on the day of his hysterical attack. In fact, her story was so difficult to tell that it required all three brothers—and Faulkner: "And I tried first to tell it with one brother, and that wasn't enough. That was Section One. I tried with another brother, and that wasn't enough. That was Section Two. I tried the third brother. . . . And that failed and I tried myself. . . ."[12] The four parts are versions of the same story: Caddy. They are somewhat like the books of Matthew, Mark, Luke, and John. One can be read without the others, but all four should be read. Benjy's story, then, is one of four.

Realizing the advantages of having an idiot tell part of *The Sound and the Fury,* Faulkner explained how he began with the nothingness, the *tabula rasa,* of Benjy's mind: ". . . the idea struck me to see how much more I could have got out of the idea of the blind, self-centeredness of innocence, typified by children, if one of those children had been truly innocent, that is, an idiot. . . . I mean 'innocence' in the sense that God had stricken him blind at birth, that is, mindless at birth. . . ."[13] Thus, with innocence, Benjy revealed the deceit, the mania for dispossession, the weight of the past, the hysteria, and, sometimes, the goodness in the characters surrounding Caddy.

In Benjy's account, Mrs. Compson and Luster and Jason revealed that mania for dispossession which Faulkner indicated had been cursing man for a long time. It was not just a trait of the Compsons or Luster. It is characteristic of history. There were Napoleon's "knightly blackguards" (p. 237). Ikkemotubbe was dispossessed by "the grandson of a Scottish refugee who had lost his own birthright by casting his lot with a king who himself had been dispossessed"

(p. 238). Even in the American Revolution, there was the retreating British army and there was the advancing American army, "both of which were wrong" (p. 239). History is repeated in *The Sound and the Fury* with dispossessed ones dispossessing the dispossessed of even small things such as a golf ball and cake.

Dispossession and deceit are not only in the past of man but in the present. However, "lessons" must always come from the past. The "lessons" of *The Sound and the Fury* are many, and there is no doubt about their being of the past. In Benjy's part alone, some thirty years wield their accumulated authority over his one day: April 7, 1928. He could not keep the thirty years at a distance. In his life, anxiety came from one day's problems which had received their top-heavy weight from the past. Ironically, the victory of the past over the present was decisive, for even the present was joined to the past by the use of the past tense: *"Cry baby, Luster said. Aint you shamed. We went through the barn. The stalls were all open. You aint got no spotted pony to ride now, Luster said"* (p. 12). The repetition of "Luster said" puts the present alongside the past of "Versh said," "Caddy said," "Dilsey said," and all other dead "said's." "Said" places all actions in the past—with "the snows of yesteryear."

The past is especially fatal to Benjy whose story by clock time lasts some twelve hours and takes place in an area restricted to the Compson house and vicinity. But his unconscious has at its beck and call some thirty years which are dissolved into one past. They are deliberately jumbled into the Versh period, the T.P. period, the Luster period, and overlapping periods. Benjy easily visited a pasture which no longer existed and heard again conversations of a faraway sister and a dead brother. All of these seemingly impossible shifts in time are possible even in the normal memory. But they are more possible in Benjy's unconscious memories on the day of his hysterical attack.

21

Another advantage in Benjy's role is his point of view as an idiot. Idiots from real life touched Faulkner and moved him to bring them into the world of fiction. Sympathy created the moron, Monk, whose origin Faulkner explained:

> I can remember a country man in my county that looked like him, who was half-witted, and possibly the story came from that. That man, a half-wit, harmless, but with no future, nothing to be done—and so possibly I tried to invent a future, even a tragic one for him, something to leave his mark on the world instead of living and dying a harmless half-imbecile.[14]

A character having more in common with Benjy is Faulkner's idiot in the story, "The Kingdom of God" (1925). Although that idiot lacks Benjy's unconscious, he is part of the whole, a part of the Kingdom of God and, like Benjy, a "part of general truth the sequence of natural events and their causes which shadows every mans brow . . ." (p. 134).

Of all Faulkner's idiots, Benjy has the most demanding role. Although he could not talk, he could moan in mortal fear of the shadows which blackened his world after the departure of his sister, Caddy. To keep her memory alive and even to bring her back, he insisted on having a grand funeral with jimson weeds in a bottle—that is, his "graveyard." But Benjy had to live according to the general truth which shadows every man's brow and, in hysteria, had to moan "on" his sister all the days of his life.[15]

# CHAPTER IV

# Samuel Beckett's Lucky: Damned

Gathering fuel in vacant lots.

—*T. S. Eliot*

In the First Act of *Waiting for Godot*, Lucky is dumb except for a macabre monologue. He is really on his philosophical deathbed. In the Second Act, he leaves behind his philosophical estate: a hat. Little can be done for him except to hold an inquest and autopsy.

The setting given at the beginning of the play is quite natural: "A country road. A tree. Evening."[1] At different times, the tree is designated by terms indicating sadness, loneliness, and smallness: a willow, a bush, a shrub. It is still day. And the road, "the road is free to all" (p. 16). But it goes nowhere.

The tramp, Gogo (Estragon), sits the pale evening out taking off his boot for airing. He and Didi (Vladimir) are waiting for Godot. "Nothing to be done," they say and say again in the shrug of defeat.

Suddenly, Lucky is driven on stage by Pozzo cracking his whip:

| POZZO: | . . . I am Pozzo! . . . |
| ESTRAGON: | . . . Bozzo . . . Bozzo . . . |
| VLADIMIR: | . . . Pozzo . . . Pozzo . . . |
| POZZO: | *PPPOZZZO!* (p. 15) |

23

The noisy rimery establishes the name as "Pozzo." However, at first, Gogo and Didi think that Pozzo is the person for whom they are waiting if only they can recall the name— yes, Godot! But no, Pozzo makes it clear that he is Pozzo and very important as he pulls hard on the rope around Lucky's neck and orders, "Up pig! . . . Up hog!" (p. 16).

Lucky rushes to follow every command. He picks up the baggage, stops and turns at Pozzo's shouts, and holds the whip in his mouth. Like a trained animal, he becomes the center of attraction and, by all dramatic rights, should carry the action forward. He does, if the action is called what it should be called: deterioration. From this point, Lucky and the other characters sink more and more. After each peripety of carrot, turnip, boot, leaf on tree, and message from Godot, the action declines.

Lucky has not always been an abused, enslaved simpleton. Sixty years ago, he knew "beautiful things," according to Pozzo (p. 22). Sixty years ago would be yesterday for Pozzo. His memory does not just go back fifty, sixty, a hundred years. There is something of man's million years (p. 7). Pozzo and Lucky's relationship is timeless and now master-slave habit. Their combined career places them in history.

There is the possibility that Pozzo is Godot because the tramps mistake Pozzo for Godot and also because Pozzo seems to know who Godot is. Yet to believe that Pozzo is Godot requires more proof than is found in the play. It is obvious that Godot is always present in the hopes of the tramps and in the title, *Waiting for Godot*. Even so, he never appears. He never sends a distinct message. He never knows that the tramps are not Mr. Albert.

Most likely, he addresses them in mockery as "Mr. Albert," meaning "bright" and "illustrious." Or, there is the chance of his good intentions and politeness when he sends a message to bright and illustrious Gogo and Didi. However, for the time being, it seems safe to say that he does not know the tramps at all. He never keeps his supposed appointment with them on a country road, near a tree, as evening approaches. The only certain conclusion is that he cannot be known by the company he keeps. He can be known only by the company he does not keep. He always remains unknown, unseen. For many reasons, it does not seem possible that Godot is Pozzo.

Perhaps centuries ago Pozzo knew Godot and met Lucky for the first time. Pozzo claims a godly lineage. He is Atlas, son of Jupiter, and has plenty of slaves like Lucky (p. 21). Jupiter or Zeus was the "father of gods and men," according to Homer. Now Zeus had children: Athena, Apollo, Artemis, Ares, Aphrodite, Hermes, Persephone, and others. But Atlas? Which of Zeus' wives bore Atlas? None. Then Atlas (Pozzo) cannot be the real son of Jupiter; at the most, he is only "son" in a figurative sense and that relationship would hardly entitle him to slaves.

Furthermore, when Pozzo states that he is Atlas, son of Jupiter, there is the implication that the supposed father-son relationship is cordial. But in Greek mythology, Atlas fought his "cousin" Zeus (both being grandsons of Uranus) in the great war between the Titan dynasty and the Olympians. Atlas was among the defeated and punished. But no punishment is suggested in Pozzo's haughty, deceitful self-description: Atlas, son of Jupiter.

"Atlas," "Jupiter," and "Pozzo" are meaningless names to Didi and Gogo who have little historical or philosophical perspective. Gogo in the First Act did say that he was Adam and in the Second Act that Pozzo was Cain and Abel. But on the whole, Gogo and Didi have little imagination as to what is beyond man's logic or beyond the "noses on their faces." The two are dead to the core. They will not see any point in the nightmarish, philosophical playlet to be presented by Lucky before their very eyes.

It would be useless for Pozzo to explain to them who he really is. Besides, such an explanation is not in keeping with his long-established habit. Probably many times he has exulted in saying that he is Atlas, son of Jupiter, or even, the son of God. He does not say that "the great dragon was cast down, the old serpent, he that is called the Devil and Satan, the deceiver of the whole world." He does not admit having connections with Adam or Cain. He does not explain that *pozzo* is the Italian word for "well," "mine shaft," and "dungeon for slaves." He never associates *pozzo* with the bottom of Dante's hell where there is "un pozzo assai largo e profondo" (XVIII,5) and a "pozzo scuro" (XXXII, 16). He does not brag about kinship with Hades or Pluto. He does not connect himself in any way with the revolt of the Titans against Zeus, the fall of Atlas, the rebellion of the angels against Jehovah, or with the fall of the rebel archangel. Yet, he has been a deceitful adventurer down through long centuries of man's existence.

So why should he now say that he is Lucifer, Beelzebub, Pluto, Hades, or Satan? That never was customary with him. And beginning late in the nineteenth century, he began to look like almost any man, as he did in *The Brothers Karamazov*: "This was a person, or more accurately speaking, a Russian gentleman. . . . The visitor's check trousers were of excellent cut, but were too light in color and too tight for present fashion. . . . In brief, there was every appearance of gentility on straitened means. . . ."[2] This Russian gentleman is the Devil who in twentieth-century literature continues to be a discreet but important figure. The role of the Devil, André Gide wrote, is essential, for *"there is no true work of art in which the collaboration of the Devil is not present."*[3]

In the modern fashion, Pozzo no longer has his horns, tail, and cloven hoofs. He has magnanimous gestures, glasses, pipe, watch, bowler, and heart-trouble. But inwardly, there is something bitter—perhaps memories of his ancient defeat by Zeus and his fall from being the highest and most perfect of angels. There is something which makes him speak sneeringly of Godot as "Godet . . . Godot . . . Godin . . ."

26

(p. 19). *Godin* with its *-in* sound is the height of a sneer. The trilogy, *Godet, Godot, Godin,* recalls *Foriot, Moriot, Loriot,* used by Balzac's haughty Duchesse de Langeais as she *tried* to recall the lowly name of Père Goriot.

This is Pozzo, master of many slaves and of old Lucky whose knowledge he had at one time admired just as Mephistopheles admired Faust for his extreme intelligence and lucidity. To prove their ages, Pozzo makes Lucky show his long, white hair. In contrast, Pozzo is a young, bald-headed man of sixty or so (p. 22). Lucky is as old as man, no doubt. Stories of good luck, bad luck, fill folklore. For example, Zeus gave man a casket containing Good Luck. Among Greek goddesses is Tyche, "chance," and the Romans had Fortuna. Fortune (Lucky) and Pozzo (Devil) have a long story.

However, only the present seems to be in the minds of Didi and Gogo as they look at Lucky's slobber and slaver and at the running sore on his neck. They hold Pozzo responsible. Didi explodes in anger, saying to Pozzo: "To treat a man . . . like that . . . I think that . . . no . . . a human being . . . no . . . it's a scandal!" (p. 18). Pushing the matter even to interrogation, Gogo asks Pozzo why Lucky does not put down the bags he is carrying.

To this question, Pozzo objectively and soothingly answers: "Has he not the right to? Certainly he has. It follows that he doesn't want to" (p. 21). In Pozzo's liberalized hell, Lucky is free to drop the bags. But he insists on keeping them, even though they are filled with sand. The sand represents heaviness, aridity, and especially eternity—eternity described by Saint-John Perse in *Anabase* as "eternity which yawns on the sands." But beyond any desire to carry sand or dead ideas, there is Lucky's wish to please Pozzo. At least that is what Pozzo claims: "He wants to impress me, so that I'll keep him" (p. 21).

To remain with Pozzo is to stay in a hell which has something from all hells—especially those of the Bible, the *Odys-*

27

*sey,* Dante's *Inferno,* and Spenser's *Faerie Queene,* and Sartre's *Huis clos.* In Pozzo's hell, there are ditches ("bolge" in Dante); beatings; noises; murky twilight; foul smells; and eating without ever reaching satisfaction. The tree is important for the setting (the Golden Bough in the *Aeneid).* There is a river (Gogo had drowned himself in the Rhone); in myths, the journey to the Otherworld is nearly always over a river or sea. Beckett has also a dog, certainly not so frightening as the three-headed, serpent-tailed Cerberus and certainly not so deeply involved in crime as Racine's Citron, guilty of coming into the kitchen and eating a fine, fat chicken, but guilty, nevertheless, of committing a crime which leads straight to hell:

> A dog came in the kitchen
> And stole a crust of bread.
> Then cook up with a ladle
> And beat him till he was dead.
>
> Then all the dogs came running
> And dug the dog a tomb— (p. 37)

Typical of hell, too, is the fate of the damned person to carry eternally his story. In *Waiting for Godot,* the most detailed eternal story is Lucky's monologue. In addition but in briefer form, there is the story of Didi who shouts "STOP IT!" as Gogo tells about the brothel (p. 11). Apparently Didi had killed someone, thereby gaining entrance to hell, and the murder may have been at the brothel. To torture Didi, Gogo says: "The best thing would be to kill me, like the other" (p. 40). Gogo, himself, probably had entered hell by having drowned himself in the Rhone (p. 35). Gogo and Didi know each other's story and, like Sartre's characters in *Huis clos,* each punishes the other by naggingly reminding him of a painful past.

Hell was defined by Beckett in 1929 in his first printed

28

work: "Hell is the static lifelessness of unrelieved viciousness."[4] This is not quite the description of Beckett's hell in 1952 in *Waiting for Godot*. There is "viciousness" but it is not "static." It is active; it is "on the loose"; it has no competition or resistance from opposing forces. It is ever-present in the characters' minds, and the "viciousness" is particularly in the memory of the other person.

For example, Lucky's story has been heard time and time again by Pozzo who is dejected and disgusted at hearing it recited once more. Although Pozzo is distressed each time he hears Lucky's story, he probably uses it to taunt him. The crisis in Lucky's past life has been a refusal. "He refused once," says Pozzo who immediately falls into silence (p. 26). Gogo and Didi insist on knowing more about Lucky's refusal but Pozzo avoids a reply by saying, "with pleasure, with pleasure" (p. 27). He merely means that he does not intend to reply. Pozzo is not protecting Lucky; he is protecting Pozzo. The refusal—whatever it was—undoubtedly involved Pozzo, too. Again, there is hell coming from the torturing telltale. No details are revealed about Lucky's refusal. But refusal and disobedience have been in man's story from the beginning when Adam preferred to obey Satan rather than God. Disobedience caused Adam to fall and Satan to remain damned.

Lucky's refusal is not any particular refusal but an important repeated refusal—Adam's—from the beginning of time. Actually, Pozzo is not Satan but all concepts of Satan and evil, while Gogo and Didi are just the world's long list of waiters. Lucky, in the role of refuser, takes the general step taken after refusal: he accepts whatever he has refused. He surrenders his mind and accepts truth as set forth in his monologue, "The Net." Thoroughly convinced and thoroughly "brain washed," he, unlike Descartes, has as his *cogito*: I do not doubt. "Beyond a doubt," he accepts everything "for reasons unknown" (pp. 28-29).

In his philosophical monologue, he stutters when he

reaches certain key words. "*Qua,*" that philosophical term meaning "in so far as," "in the capacity of," and "in the function of" and indicating that the philosopher has to compromise by using terms which are not "absolute" and even has to wait for "Godot"—"*qua*" causes Lucky to stutter "quaquaquaqua" (p. 28). This phenomenal repetition brings out not only the first meaning of "*qua*" but second and third meanings: "farthing" and, in the language of thieves, "prison."[5]

The several meanings of another word, "academy," are not lost in Lucky's pronunciation: "Acacacacademy" (p. 28). There are august academies of men of science, letters, and arts. There are academies or brothels. There are academies to give thieves their proper schooling as, for example, the one in the Middle Ages in Paris where the pocket of a dummy, suspended on a cord and covered with thousands of little bells, had to be "picked" without sounding one of the bells by the "candidate" for the "Master's."[6] At least one more meaning is emphasized in "Acacacacademy" and that is *cacare,* "to void excrement." A more difficult word to pronounce is "Anthropopopometry" (p. 28) because it has not only "anthropometry" but also "popo" which suggests "popomatic" and especially "po," a word used in the expression, "full as a po" and meaning "extremely drunk."

After stuttering, Lucky begins to prove his philosophy by citing authorities: Belcher, Peterman, Clapham, Fulham, *et al* (pp. 28-29). These are not always proper nouns in the English language. Often, they are very common nouns: "belcher" is a "hard drinker of beer" and, in the language of thieves, "a ring"; "peterman" is "one who uses unlawful means to catch fish in the Thames" or "one who specializes in stealing bags from carriages"; "clapham" is found in the expression, "he went out by Had'em and come home by Clapham" which means "he went out a-wenching and got a clap"—gonorrhoea; "fulham" is used in "high fulham," a die loaded for a cast of 4, 5, or 6, and in "low fulham," a

30

die loaded for a cast of 1, 2, or 3. If the authority, Fulham, has any connections with "high and low fulhams," he is a man who wants to be certain "beyond all doubt" and for reasons known by him but, of course, unknown by others. Philosophers in Lucky's system want to be certain and, for them, there is the philosophical city, "Essy-in-Possy" (p. 28), magnificent in built-in contradictions: *esse* for *in esse,* "in actual existence," and *in posse,* "in potentiality." Philosophers, men high and low, all men, and Lucky would like to know "beyond all doubt." Nevertheless, Lucky's memorized theses have fragments, containing their own destruction and the destruction of various philosophies from "six hundred and something" to the age of "all sorts penicilline" (p. 29). His recitation recalls Pascal's *Provinciales* where word is turned against word and contradiction against contradiction.

The exaggerated dependence upon authority is Lucky's means of showing that he accepts without questioning. There will never again be refusal or disobedience on his part. He has learned his lesson. The result is inanity, for Lucky is "alas alas abandoned unfinished the skull the skull . . ." (p. 29). He has almost reached perfect rigidity and order, the dream of another Beckett character, Clov: "I love order. It's my dream. A world where all would be silent and still and each thing in its last place, under the last dust."[7] When this point is reached, life, not death, is the great leveler.

Lucky's thought is soon to be in its final resting place, for Pozzo suffers so greatly that he orders Gogo and Didi to seize Lucky's hat. Without his hat, Lucky instantly stops his philosophizing. This time, Pozzo wants to be certain that Lucky "thinks" no more; he throws the hat to ground, tramples it, and shouts: "There's an end to his thinking!" (p. 30). Pozzo can no longer bear being bored by Lucky's skeletal ideas which he describes in the fashion of a proverb: "In theory the bones go to the carrier" (p. 18). What Pozzo wants to do with Lucky and his philosophical "bones" and bags of sand is to sell him at the fair. But somehow Pozzo ironically has the habit of enduring him and does not sell him.

Characters of easy prey like Lucky, Gogo ("Sucker"), and Didi ("Twin") are weaklings and offer no challenge to Pozzo who has the personality of the Devil described by Paul Valéry: "The Devil said: 'That man was not intelligent enough for me to bother to argue with. He didn't have enough wit. . . . He didn't understand a jot or tittle of my temptation.' "[8] Valéry's devil and Beckett's devil are rather alike in their feeling of superiority. But Pozzo does not wait until his victim has gone to speak of his stupidity. He insults Lucky to his face by calling him "hog," "pig," and "scum." Directly he says to Gogo and Didi: "You know how to think, you two?" (p. 26). Once with great generosity he remarked to Gogo: "From the meanest creatures one departs wiser, richer, more conscious of one's blessings. Even you . . . even you, who knows, will have added to my store" (p. 20). Gogo, Didi, and Lucky are unbearable to Pozzo. But he must converse with them and even take charge of these beings who by his indulgence are "human beings none the less" (p. 15).

These "human beings" who are so distasteful to Pozzo come his way because he, the Devil, deliberately has placed himself in their paths. Long ago, he knew that his defiance of the gods would place him in hell. He was conscious of his destiny and accepted it. Pozzo is certain that he is destined to be of no help to the "damned" ones like Lucky, Gogo, and Didi, but he does not have time to regret his useless profession. Speaking of his responsibility toward them, he says: "Is there anything I can do, that's what I ask myself, to cheer them up? I have given them bones, I have talked to them about this and that, I have explained the twilight, admittedly. But is it enough, that's what tortures me, is it enough?" (p. 26). This is Pozzo in his ugly, useless work. But with courage, he pursues his role of deceit to the very limit of possibility. At the end of the play, he is weak and stumbling, but he continues whipping Lucky. He and Lucky both are damned to repetition—to habit.

Habit, Time, and Memory are found in an essay published by Beckett in 1931 and entitled *Proust*. In that essay, Beckett imagined the "Proustian equation" as being "Memory and Habit are attributes of the Time cancer."[9] The tragedy of the human condition in *Waiting for Godot* and in Beckett's other work comes from Time aided by Memory and Habit. His Lucky is a dying example.

Preceding and following Lucky are other Beckettian creatures who could well be called "Luckies." They are hapless examples of the immobility and paralysis of the living. Some cannot sit down; some cannot stand; some have lost their legs; some cannot move; one is buried to her waist in a sand pile and as the action progresses, she is buried up to her neck. Definitely, something is amiss with the living in Beckett's characters, for they are so halted by Habit, Time, and Memory and so deadened in body that they must be placed in wheel chairs, locked in bins, or confined to a sand pile. Even though they have names such as Didi, Gogo, Hamm, Clov, Nagg, Nell, Winnie, Willie, Pim, Bem, and one is just *the man*, they seem to belong to the Don't-Move family. They are as related to each other as the Rougons are to the Macquarts, the Kallikaks to the Kallikaks, and the Snopeses to the Snopeses. They are "Luckies."

They have at least one philosophic progenitor, Henri Bergson and his theory of "the mechanical encrusted upon the living."[10] If the living is not changing without ceasing and being built up each instant with its accumulated experiences, it is dead and mechanical. When the living falls under the domination of matter (Habit), it becomes inelastic and comic. In the same way, man becomes a puppet, a marionette, and even a thing.

Lucky does not change, he is dead. He is, in fact, comic on the stage. But his comedy is black. In life, he was "dead" and now is forever dead in hell. An autopsy of the causes

33

of death is held in the monologue with its leitmotiv, "it is established beyond all doubt." This monologue had become his comfortable way of thinking while he was living. "Habit," Beckett wrote, "is a compromise effected between the individual and his environment, . . . the guarantee of a dull inviolability, the lightning-conductor of his existence. Habit is the ballast that chains the dog to his vomit."[11]

It can be seen that Lucky escaped the dangerous thrill of thinking by memorizing quotations and then quoting them in fragments. Finally, he had a long philosophical discourse which he could recite at any time without mental effort or risk. This discourse, which he recites in *Waiting for Godot*, had become years ago a conductor to lead safely away any "electric" ideas. It had become habit. Even Didi and Gogo know the danger of habit which Didi describes in rare metaphor: "Down in the hole, lingeringly, the grave-digger put on the forceps. We have time to grow old. The air is full of our cries. But habit is a great deadener" (p. 58).

One of these habits which Didi and Gogo discuss is thought. They view man's thought as being full of corpses and skeletons which come from the tomb, from "a charnel house! A charnel house!" (p. 41). Thoughts are from the tomb as long as they come from voluntary memory, as with Lucky. Involuntary memory might have made Lucky's thought living and allowed him to grasp some essence. It is involuntary memory which is "explosive" according to Beckett. Involuntary memory "in its flame . . . has consumed Habit and all its works, and in its brightness revealed what the mock reality of experience never can and never will reveal—the real."[12] Lucky's voluntary memory will never take him to the real but will keep him in the false world of habit.

Time is also against Lucky. No matter what success he has attained as a philosophical puppet, it will all be swept away by Time. The theme of Time appears and reappears in *Waiting for Godot*. Didi has a problem in the appointment with Godot who, he thinks, is to come Saturday. Gogo doubtingly asks: "But what Saturday? And is it Saturday? Is it not rather Sunday? . . . Or Monday? . . . Or Friday?" (p. 11). Gogo wonders whether Godot will know about man's Saturday, but Didi just understands small-time living and has no concept of Time.

Pozzo understands Time even though he seems to prefer the time of his watch, "a genuine half-hunter . . . with dead-beat escapement!" (p. 30). His awareness of Time is revealed in answer to Didi's pronouncement that "Time has stopped" (p. 24). Immediately, Pozzo disagrees: "Don't you believe it, Sir, don't you believe it. Whatever you like but not that" (p. 24). Pozzo knows that Time does not allow the permanent establishment of anything—not even of hell where the characters find themselves and, even there, sink. The lowest point of the downward action is reached in the last line of the play when Didi says to Gogo: "Yes, let's go" (p. 60). They do not move. Lucky descended to that lowly point long before the others. After his recitation filled with the onomatopoeia of sterility, there is nothing for him except muteness—damnation. Beckett's formula holds: "Memory and Habit are attributes of the Time cancer."

# CHAPTER V

# Günter Grass's Oskar: the Rogue

[Modern genius] changes giants
into dwarfs. . . .
                                    —*Victor Hugo*

No hero from Don Juan to Little Abner ever upset life's tranquility more than Günter Grass's Oskar. In appearance, Oskar was a three-year-old child. In action, he was a little rogue who surfaced often from propaganda rallies, battles, streets, and boudoir scenes "to get an eye full." Evaluations and explanations of his findings could lead to allegory, irony, parody, satire, character assassinations, and any type of literature which destroys. But perhaps imagining Oskar in the roles of Oskar-Lazarillo, Oskar-Proust, and Oskar-Philosopher will not limit too seriously the multiple interpretations he deserves.

Oskar never called himself "Lazarillo" or *picaro,* "rogue," but his early decision for deceit marks him as a precocious rogue, a twentieth-century kinsman of Lazarillo and Guzmán de Alfarache and the fellow countryman of Till Eulenspiegel and Simplicius.

On his third birthday, he received a drum. At once, he resolved to remain three feet tall, to wear the same style sailor suit, and always to have a child's drum so that he could be the eternal three-year-old.[1] His success in fraud was complete, for who would believe that Oskar was sixteen to twenty-one years old in the following descriptions. "A little brat, who must have been about three, pounded monotonously on a child's tin drum, turning the afternoon into an infernal smithy. . . ."[2] There was "something about a three-year-old child whom the gang had cherished as a kind of mascot."[3] Someone noticed that "a little boy who might have been three years old, didn't want to be connected with the grandmothers, and was carrying but not beating a child's drum."[4] The "little boy" seen here and there is Oskar in the novel, *Cat and Mouse* (1961).

Casual observers mentioned him in *Dog Years*, a novel published in 1963.[5] But in *The Tin Drum* (1959), no one had to talk for Oskar; he talked for himself as he drummed back his memories. His adventures in three novels add authenticity to his career as rogue and technically make him a reappearing character of the type invented by Balzac in 1833 and used by the French author for the first time in *Le Père Goriot* (1834). Reappearances create an Oskar whose own tall tales become even taller through the chance remarks of others.

Understandably, the person who talked most about Oskar was Oskar. Yet what he said about himself in *The Tin Drum* is not too important, for he is no great character of goodness, evil, or a happy combination. What little others said about him is not essential even though exciting and lurid. But what is important is what Oskar saw, heard, and was just "dying" to report.

Preferring to visit various persons—the *picaro* would have said preferring one master after another—Oskar determined to remain free of "five-foot-eight adulthood."[6] He was quick to realize that school was a step in the wrong direction. One day there was enough. To insist on his unfitness for school, he screamed in such a high-pitched voice that he shattered windows and broke the lens of the teacher's glasses when she took his drum away from him. Generally he let out a fierce, glass-breaking scream whenever anyone took his drum. Later, he used this miraculous power to break shop windows. Since he did not go to school, he went with Mama once a week to meet Bronski in a hotel room.

Another visit Oskar made often was to Meyn who, when drunk, could play the trumpet too beautifully for words. Later Oskar spent considerable time retelling the story about Meyn: "There was once a musician, his name was Meyn, and if he isn't dead he is still alive, once again playing the trumpet too beautifully for words" (p. 206). This sentence with slight variations and ever-so-little progress in thought is repeated and repeated in a parody of philosophical style—especially of Kierkegaard's interpretations of the story of Abraham.

Oskar (1924-    ) at the beginning of the Second World War was fifteen years old and in a lovely position to enjoy it. He was completely free. No military service. No job. No school.[7] But he did not compromise his duty as rogue, for he attended Party and Hitler Youth rallies by hiding under rostrums, and he "huddled under the rostrum for Reds and Blacks, for Boy Scouts and Spinach Shirts, for Jehovah's Witnesses, the Kyffhäuser Bund, the Vegetarians, and the Young Polish Fresh Air Movement. Whatever they might have to sing, trumpet, or proclaim, [his] drum knew better" (p. 124). Happily, during the Polish Campaign, he spent his time at the Polish Post Office and City Hospital. Then he followed the battles of the Second World War by radio until 1942 when he became quite active in the war effort because he no doubt wanted to have some service before the war was over. That year, he joined a midget group to entertain the German Army of Occupation in France. But things in France simply did not go well for him. There were bombings, shellings. He had to leave. Back in Danzig, he found things better and as "I am Jesus" helped lead a hoodlum, teen-age gang, the "Dusters." Things got bad in Danzig. There were the police. Then, the Russians.

But Oskar, rogue, was quite capable of meeting any situation. He fled. Therefore, when the Russians came, he left Danzig with refugees, spent some time in a hospital in Hanover, and then a longer time in a hospital in Düsseldorf. When conditions became better in Düsseldorf, Oskar got better and was able to leave the hospital. In fact, he had begun to grow after having left Danzig, and now he was four feet-one and among the able bodied. He found a job cutting inscriptions on tombstones—a thriving business.

However, there was some unexpected personal irony in carving inscriptions on tombstones, something sad. Oskar began to become fond of cutting the letter *O*. Then he had a dream about "Here lies Oskar" (p. 446). The typical *picaro* belief in predestination was setting in. Not long afterwards, Oskar agreed with Klepp that men are born by mistake and are doomed to die (p. 503). By this time, Oskar had had considerable experience from which to deduce the idea of chance. He had posed in the nude at the Academy of Art; had organized a jazz band for the Onion Cellar; and had even become a solo performer billed as "Oskar, the Drummer." All these acts are those in which the individual would like to become a hero.

But dwarfs and giants and individuals are not quite sure of themselves in the twentieth century. Even Oskar is not the hero of a novel called *Oskar;* he is merely in *The Tin Drum* and in the world where there are "little people and big people, Little Claus and Great Claus, Tiny Tim and Carolus Magnus, David and Goliath, Jack the Giant Killer and, of course, the giant" (p. 60). There is no real difference between smallness and largeness in man's condition where the contraries of dwarf and giant coincide. Oskar could just as easily have willed to be a giant. But gigantic size would not have made him stronger than the "gnome, the Tom Thumb, the pigmy, the Lilliputian, the midget" (p. 60) that he was. No one could have been more conscious of the impossibility of heroism than Oskar as he looked at

Velásquez' court paintings with dwarfs the size of "Oskar, in ruffs, goatees, and baggy pantaloons" (p. 308).

His hard look was directed more toward others whom he saw struggling in domestic scenes, petty businesses, schools, war, cemeteries, and in all imaginable and unimaginable tactics. His observations were bitter and cynical: "An entire credulous nation believed, there's faith for you, in Santa Claus. But Santa Claus was really the gasman" (p. 203). There is Oskar's story about the S. A. trooper who attempted to kill four cats and was immediately called to court for inhuman cruelty to animals (p. 201). Then after the war, Oskar noticed an increase in resistance fighters (those who had resisted the Nazi Party) because there were included those who had "resisted" by not blacking out their windows during the war.

Certainly, evidence can be found to show that Oskar lacked faith in man, doubted good fate, and realized full well that living from pillar to post is not true freedom. As a twentieth-century rogue, he was well-provided with passports, but those passports gave him no easier, no happier adventures than those of Lazarillo and Simplicius. Really, he was irritated with man so content to travel within the bounds permitted by passports: "O man amid snapshots, passport photos. O man beneath the glare of flash bulbs, O man standing erect by the leaning tower of Pisa, O photomaton man who must expose his right ear if he is to be worthy of a passport!" (p. 50).

A journey unknown to the old-fashioned rogue was to the past over the route of memory. But Oskar was eager to travel anywhere twentieth-century man could go. If that included Proust's "immense edifice of memory,"[8] then Oskar wanted to go there. So it was that he used memory to make many connections in his triple personality: *I, Mr. Matzerath,* and *Oskar.*

*I, Mr. Matzerath,* and *Oskar* present one and the same

40

character with as much confusion as possible. The three persons succeed in making contradictions more contradictory by adding new contradictions before old ones are cleared up. *I* is usually limited to the time when the character was thirty years old, respectable, and uninteresting. *Mr. Matzerath* is the subject of Bruno's brief report written at the character's request while in the mental hospital. Bruno began in law-like, deposition style: "I, Bruno Münsterberg, of Altena in Sauerland, unmarried and childless, am a male nurse in the private pavilion of the local mental hospital" (p. 419). The contents of this report are: first, Bruno's identification, legally so essential; and secondly, Oskar's false, impressive statements to be left behind as his worthy history.

*Oskar* is the part enjoyed by Oskar. Here he recalled memories of his role as a professional three-year-old child and relived with delight all the futility and stupidity he had found in adults. Knowing that all the details of his memory would become extensive "history," Oskar sent for a ream of paper on which to record them. His first memory went back to a Monday in October 1899 when Grandmother was sitting in the slanting rain near a Kashubian potato fire. Suddenly a man pursued by police appeared and was hidden by Grandmother. That day, the man became Grandfather Koljaiczek. Oskar's story began with his grandparents in 1899. It ended with them in 1954 when he would have gone to Grandmother had there not been the Iron Curtain or he would have travelled to Grandfather in Buffalo, U.S.A. had there not been the Black Witch: "Ha! ha! ha!" (p. 589).

Just how could Oskar who was born in 1924 recall the potato field of 1899? His drum made it possible: ". . . if I didn't have the permission of the management to drum on it three or four hours a day, I'd be a poor bastard with nothing to say for my grandparents" (p. 25). Since Oskar could recall twenty-five years more than he had lived, his method was more successful than that of Freud who expected

41

his patients to reveal only their own long-forgotten, suppressed experiences, and he recalled more than Proust who by means of the famous madeleine steeped in tea could bring back lost time only from his lifetime. Oskar was a genius in being able to remember years he had not even lived.

Those past years were recalled without the use of Proustian fetishes, such as, a musty smell, noise of a spoon against a plate, or the gurgle of water in pipes. All that Oskar needed was his drum which put control, will, and spite into his remembrance of things past. As he drummed back his past, he tormented all those present to their wit's end. They could not snatch the drum away from him, because he would shriek. He had his audience at his mercy. Perhaps enjoyment of his annoying power kept him from having time to savor the sensations, view the nuances, and penetrate all the emotions associated with memories.

But lingering memories might have filled Oskar with nostalgia for the past. This is the exact opposite of Oskar's fictional role which is to ridicule the past (1899-1954). But more serious than Oskar's laughing bitterly at the past is his criticism of the easy, comfortable way of cleaning up the past by placing it under tombstones with neatly cut inscriptions of "Here lies so and so," a noble way to bury man's mistakes and ironically place them so as to be honored with flowers on special occasions. Oskar wanted to look into many lightly and hastily covered graves of the immediate past. If they were shallow enough, the stench would come to the surface. For the purpose of uncovering as many places and people as possible, Oskar did not want to take time to exhume the most deeply buried but wanted to throw open thousands of the shallowest graves. Oskar, reputation robber, preferred to dig up as much error as possible, but he did not want to dig far below the surface.

He found the years 1899 to 1954 unsuitable for the deep penetration of the inner monologue, for example, of Joyce.

For Oskar, an hour is sixty seconds, each second armed with an alarming message from the past. His hour could not be Proust's hour, a "vase filled with perfumes, sounds, projects, and climates." This kind of hour for the years 1899-1954 would require reams and reams of paper, and Oskar had bought only one ream. By necessity and intention, his memories are brief and many. It is best for him to remember information about a certain forty or sixty-watt light bulb, headlines about the stock market crash in New York, and other facts. Oskar's memories are shallow, for he is not a hero but a rogue of the unconscious.

He is a satirist, but no more of Proust than of any writer who finds connections between man and things, who discovers correspondences (*correspondances* of Baudelaire, for instance), or who believes that things and nature change to match man's sadness and happiness (pathetic fallacy). Oskar recalled things: shipyards, dry docks, scrap metal dumps, pee soup (not pea soup), the doctor's collection of snakes, toads, and embryos. He recalled places: Danzig, Poland, the opera-in-the-woods, the beach. He recalled people: Klepp, Jan Bronski, Stephan Bronski, Gretchen, Bebra, Grandmother, Roswitha, and others. But things were things, places were places, and people were people. He kept each mental entry in a separate place: "The ability to drum the necessary distance between grownups and myself developed shortly after my fall," (p. 64) explained Oskar.

Deliberately, he made no philosophical analogies or connections. To prevent the merging of things, places, and people, he recalled them singly on his tin drum, an instrument producing one shallow beat after another. His tin drum could not sonorously and feelingly play many themes at once: the symphony of Flaubert's country fair in *Madame Bovary* or the fugue of Gide's *Faux-Monnayeurs*. On Oskar's drum, the facts came back one at a time and right-side up (no one side and its reverse as in *L'Envers et l'endroit* of Camus).

The language of his drum is simple in vocabulary and flat in imagination. There are no metaphors, the glory of Proust. There are no gigantic leaps of the imagination to connect profoundly Oskar and things, Oskar and places, and Oskar and people. To get information about his grandfather's drowning or not drowning, Oskar set forth his method: "It's not easy, with nothing better than a tin drum, the kind you can buy in the dimestore, to question a river clogged nearly to the horizon with log rafts" (p. 37). It was through the tin drum that Oskar found again the littered surfaces of past time.

If his drum gave forth no metaphors, if there was no depth of feeling and analysis, this does not mean that there was no philosophy. Oskar's ticker-tape prose clicked off considerable philosophy. He was a city-urchin philosopher. Like Candide, he encountered the worst of possible worlds. Yet his real discovery was man in existence (Being, Time, and Nothing) and, if pinned down, he would have probably supported Heidegger's statement that "Being and Nothing hang together . . . because Being itself is finite in essence and is only revealed in the Transcendence of *Da-sein* as projected into Nothing."[9] Heidegger's thought in Oskar's practical language might have been: Roguery and the Black Witch hang together because Roguery itself is finite in essence and is only revealed in the Transcendence of Existence as projected into the Black Witch. Oskar certainly was busy trying to find something with his drumming, and perhaps philosophically it was: Roguery is Being; the Black Witch is Nothing.

Puzzled by the Black Witch, Oskar said: "Don't ask Oskar who she is! Words fail me. First she was behind me, later she kissed my hump, but now and forever, she is in front of me, coming closer" (p. 589). For a non-philosopher, Oskar conducted his thought admirably. To the point was his observation that the Black Witch occupied two positions:

44

she had been behind him; then she was in front of him. When she was behind him, she was pushing: she was race, moment, and milieu; she was Grandmother Koljaiczek in the potato patch; Grandfather Koljaiczek, fire-bug, voluntary fireman, and later a multimillionaire, a "big stockholder in a number of match factories, a founder of fire insurance companies" (p. 37); she was Danzig; moths around the light bulb; the grocery store; she was even Rasputin whom Oskar admired but had to call childishly "Rashu! Rashu!" From the past, the Black Witch was determining his future.

But in front of him, she represented rather aggressive finalism since she came toward him. Oskar, trapped between determinism and finalism—a possible philosophical position —sang a back song:

> Always behind me, the Black Witch.
> Now ahead of me, too, facing me, Black.
> Black words, black coat, black money.
> But if children sing, they sing no longer:
> Where's the Witch, black as pitch?
> Here's the black, wicked Witch.
> Ha! ha! ha! (p. 589)

This comic yet lyric poem put "black" behind and before Oskar. Every direction was black so that his Roguery (Being) could not be distinguished from the Black Witch (Nothing). The two fused.

They illustrate, if folklore can, Hegel's conclusion that "Pure Being and Pure Nothing are thus the one and the same."[10] At thirty, Oskar woke up to the fact of philosophical oneness; but oneness had begun when he was zero age minus twenty-four; thirty was only the shocking moment of identifying blackness, of recognizing the "mode of existence the thirty-year-old Oskar is planning to carry on in the shadow of a bugaboo which, though getting blacker and blacker, is the same old friend that used to frighten [him] . . ." (p. 588). Being and Nothing and the forces, determinism and finalism, had existed all along in his life under the guise of Roguery and the Black Witch and had been those unknown things on which he had not been able to put his sly finger. In the irony of a turn-about-is-fair-play, he could not blackmail them as he had Mama, Bronski, and Matzerath who was probably his father. The "black" never came out of the shadows to negotiate with him.

His life, caught between determinism and finalism, is old-fashioned. If he is to be worth his philosophical salt in the twentieth century, he must stand up and be counted as an existentialist or essentialist. Surely existentialism (existence-before-essence) can be found in his machination to remain "the three-year-old, the gnome, the Tom Thumb, the pigmy, the Lilliputian, the midget, whom no one could persuade to grow" (p. 60). It must be remembered how he had taken his destiny in hand and on his third birthday had flung himself through a trap door which Matzerath had left open: "And so with a single fall, . . . [he] not only supplied a reason—repeatedly confirmed by the doctors and in general satisfactory to the grownups who simply must have their explanations for things—for [his] failure to grow, but in addition . . . transformed . . . harmless, good-natured Matzerath into a guilty Matzerath" (p. 63). This was the existential triumph of Oskar who for years enjoyed being free to be a three-year-old rogue. Riding upon the wave of success, he was able to become a patient in a mental hospital. To think how delighted he would have been to have had Faulkner's Luster point a finger at him and say: " 'he been three years old thirty years.' " Such an accusation would have kept Oskar permanently in the hospital where he wanted to be. When he had to leave, he knew that he could not create his own existence which would have been a future of nice hospital beds.

But he almost became a successful, practicing existen-

46

tialist. By controlling his growth and by saying "Doethe, Doethe" for "Goethe, Goethe," he appeared to be a three-year-old child. In one respect, he improved existentialism, for he attained delightful freedom rather than dreadful freedom. This happy state of affairs probably removed him from being a pure existentialist. To come to the point, it made him a false existentialist.

If he did not succeed in becoming an existentialist, then he must have been an essentialist and put essence before existence. For all practical purposes, essence in Oskar's life was determinism with several examples: on the day of his birth, a moth drummed on two sixty-watt bulbs; his mother said that day that he would receive a drum on his third birthday; and he was born clairaudient and had the ability to hear sounds not normally audible. From this essence came his existence as a drummer. Drumming was his life to the extent that he was allowed to continue drumming even in the mental hospital. Naturally, it was against his wishes to be dismissed: "Just what I have been dreading for years . . . : that they would . . . discharge me from this mental hospital, take away my lovely bed, put me out in the cold street . . ." (p. 578). They did. The shock was great. Even essence could not assure his future as a drummer.

With dread closing in, he began to think of another career: "Marry? Stay single? Emigrate? Model? Buy a stone quarry? Gather disciples? Found a sect?" (p. 587). On these decisive questions, the novel ends. Should Oskar ever found a sect, its members quite likely would be exponents of "Oskarism," a philosophy which would be neither determinism, finalism, existentialism, nor essentialism. It would be simply against man's fakery. It would have many interpretations and applications not only for Germany but for man in general.

Oskar, who appears as an annoying three-year-old brat with a drum, shatters points of view just as effectively as he did glass. This is the intention of Günter Grass who in

47

a discourse delivered October 9, 1965, at Darmstadt upon receiving the Büchner Prize, stung Germany—especially intellectual leaders—and outlined areas for criticism: ". . . it is a question of denouncing the failure of a nation; counterfeitness of a literature; the *hybris* of a personality which feels itself confirmed; the sententious ethics of a nation which does not exist."[11] Before this discourse, he had thrown into action the dwarf Oskar, armed for destruction and wearing the battle-worn uniforms of Oskar-Lazarillo, Oskar-Proust, and Oskar-Philosopher. And Oskar has never been killed in battle. He is still Oskar (1924-    ) and has the reputation of reappearing as a rogue.

# CHAPTER VI
# The Unknown of the Mind

It can be said then, that the
study of the mind is connected
with metaphysics.
—*Simone Weil*

The minds of simple fictional characters can be "read like a book." But when characters are as deep as Victor Hugo's Quasimodo, William Faulkner's Benjy, Samuel Beckett's Lucky, and Günter Grass's Oskar, their minds offer realms for exploration.

Quasimodo, Benjy, Lucky, and Oskar are not simply fantastic and grotesque like the saintly idiot, Nick, of Pushkin's *Boris Godunov* (1825) and Moussorgsky's opera, *Boris Godunov*. Their minds take them beyond the primitive, morbid idiot brothers who in Horacio Quiroga's story, "La Gallina degollada" (1917), slit their little sister's throat in a successful imitation of the cook killing a chicken.

They differ, too, from Miguel de Unamuno's idiot, Blasillo, who repeats one question in *San Manuel Bueno, Mártir* (1933): "My God, my God, why hast thou forsaken me?" They are not Steinbeck's simple-minded Lennie in *Of Mice and Men* (1937) who "loves to touch soft things such as mice, puppies, and women and leave them dead. . . ."

They represent wider philosophical interests than the half-witted, Rere, the last of a noble Hungarian family in

49

Zilahy's *The Dukays* (1949) and the symbol not only of a decadent family but of an entire continent weakened by revolutions and world wars.

They are not limited to being the terrifying, evil Cousin Lymon, created by Carson McCullers for "The Ballad of the Sad Café" (1951). Nor do they merely intensify the tragic background as does the feeble-minded "dummy," Georgie, in Saul Bellow's *The Adventures of Augie March* (1953). They are not the fanciful idiot, Simon, in Romain Weingarten's *L'Été* (1965).

Quasimodo, Benjy, Lucky, and Oskar offer more than magic, violence, terror, the fantastic, the decadent, and the tragic. They have minds developed according to a certain theory of mind. Each has his role to play so that Quasimodo's sensationalism has little connection with Benjy's unconscious which does not explain the mechanical repetition of Lucky or the cold realism of Oskar's tin-drum recollections.

Dependent upon imperfect senses, Quasimodo's mind receives few impressions from the outside world and is explained in part by the philosophy of Locke, La Mettrie, Condillac, Helvétius, and Maine de Biran. There still remains, however, the unknown of Quasimodo's mind which, Hugo imagined, would require a torch for lighting the dark recesses and a microscope for finding the minute impressions.

Replacing Hugo's fanciful microscope for the mind is Faulkner's analysis of Benjy's unconscious, brought into action by hysteria. Even though Benjy "recalls" accurately every conversation and event which his brain has recorded, there is something unknown in his pantomime of moaning and playing graveyard.

At some time in the past, Beckett's Lucky had tried to separate himself from the living and from change by accepting safe thoughts which he put into a philosophical "discourse." This is the "discourse" he repeats by memory in *Waiting for Godot* where he is in hell for the sin of mechanical thinking or for what Bergson typed "the mechanical

50

encrusted upon the living." Lucky's long-rehearsed, philosophical gibberish in the playlet within *Waiting for Godot* presents the undesirable, negative qualities of mental inertia but in no way explains why a philosophical catechism is necessary for man. Beckett, unrelentingly, established the mental fact, the inflexibility, the artificiality of his character's mind. The reality of the mind, however, is left in the unknown.

Then, Günter Grass presents Oskar in *The Tin Drum* and makes him a character who would deny the unknown and prefer to be removed from things, people, places, dangers, philosophy, and nature. Oskar enjoys alienation from the world and strives to be free from all the debris of memory which his tin drum gathers for him. It is the reader who becomes involved in Oskar's memories and who becomes furious at that little brat, at that little rogue, with such vulgar taste. Should the reader protest, Oskar would just rattle his drum and gleefully find some other skeleton in man's political and philosophical closet and play again and again his anti-philosophical role. But even Oskar cannot remain detached from nature, for in the end he fully feels the power of the Black Witch behind him and in front of him.

He joins Quasimodo, Benjy, and Lucky and, like them, lives exaggeratedly a philosophy of mind and serves as a witness to its passing. The unknown of the mind remains, and all investigation leaves the impression "of having found a locked drawer, then a key; and the key opens the drawer easily . . . and the drawer is empty."[1]

# Notes

## CHAPTER I

1. Claude-Adrien Helvétius, *Notes de la main d'Helvétius*, ed. Albert Keim (Paris: Alcan, 1907), p. 5. In this study, I have translated all French passages into English.
2. Julien Offray de La Mettrie, *Traité de l'âme*, in *Textes choisis*, ed. Marcelle Tisserand (Paris: Éditions Sociales, 1954), pp. 123-124.
3. Pierre Maine de Biran, *Influence de l'habitude sur la faculté de penser*, ed. Pierre Tisserand (Paris: Presses Universitaires de France, 1954), pp. ix-lxiv.
4. Henri Bergson, *Écrits et paroles*, ed. R.-M. Mossé-Bastide (Paris: Presses Universitaires de France, 1959), II, 424.
5. Sigmund Freud, *The Interpretation of Dreams*, in *The Basic Writings of Sigmund Freud*, ed. and trans. A. A. Brill (New York: Random House, 1938), p. 542.
6. Henri Bergson, quoted by Jean-Claude Filloux, *L'Inconscient* (Paris: Presses Universitaires de France, 1965), p. 5.
7. Eugène Ionesco, *Notes et contre-notes* (Paris: Gallimard, 1966), pp. 313-314.

## CHAPTER II

1. Victor Hugo, *Notre-Dame de Paris: 1482*, in *Oeuvres complètes*, ed. Ollendorff (Paris: L'Imprimérie Nationale, 1904), Roman II, 37. Page numbers for other references to *Notre-Dame de Paris* will appear in the text. I have translated into English all quotations from Hugo's work and from other French authors quoted in this chapter.
2. Victor Hugo, *Han d'Islande*, in *Oeuvres complètes*, ed. Ollendorff (Paris: L'Imprimérie Nationale, 1910), Roman I, 37.
3. Victor Hugo, *Cromwell*, in *Oeuvres complètes*, ed. Ollendorff (Paris: L'Imprimérie Nationale, 1912), Théâtre I, 14.
4. Victor Hugo, *Littérature et philosophie mêlées* (Paris: Hetzel et Quantin, n.d.), p. 201.
5. Géraud Venzac, *Les Premiers Maîtres de Victor Hugo* (Paris: Bloud et Gay, 1955), p. 301. Venzac's work treats the years, 1809-1818.
6. *Ibid.*, p. 307. Venzac mentions Locke also on the following pages: 314, 317, and 435.
7. Hugo, "Journal d'un jeune jacobite de 1819," in *Littérature et philosophie mêlées*, p. 114. An additional but insignificant mention of Locke

52

is found on page 43 where Hugo expressed surprise at hearing a woman quote Locke. At the end of *Littérature et philosophie mêlées* in a section entitled, "Mirabeau," Locke is mentioned as one of the sources for Mirabeau's ideas (p. 301).

8. Condillac's works, *Traité des systèmes, L'Art de penser,* and *La Logique,* were on the list of books prepared in 1809 in France for students in philosophy. See Venzac, *Les Premiers Maîtres de Victor Hugo,* p. 301 and p. 307.

9. Pierre Maine de Biran, *Influence de l'habitude sur la faculté de penser,* ed. Pierre Tisserand (Paris: Presses Universitaires de France, 1954), p. 34.

10. *Ibid.,* p. xiii.

11. Jean-Bertrand Barrère, *Hugo: l'homme et l'oeuvre* (Paris: Hatier, 1952), p. 254.

12. Hugo, *Littérature et philosophie mêlées,* p. 12. An eighteenth-century author of importance to Hugo is Diderot. However, Hugo listed rather inaccurately in *William Shakespeare* the facts of a cartoon entitled, "Diderot Being Whipped." See *Oeuvres complètes de Diderot,* ed. J. Assézat and M. Tourneux (Paris: Garnier, 1875), I, 431.

The life of Diderot ("Mémoires pour servir à l'histoire de la vie et des ouvrages de Diderot") by his daughter, Madame de Vandeul, did not appear until 1830, when it was published in *Oeuvres inédites de Diderot* (Paris: Paulin, 1830). There was also Diderot's *Oeuvres* (Paris: M. Brière, 1821). In connection with sensations and Locke's philosophy, the following works of Diderot are very important: *Lettres sur les aveugles à l'usage de ceux qui voient* (1749); *Lettres sur les sourds et muets à l'usage de ceux qui entendent et qui parlent* (1751).

For some other aspects of Hugo and the eighteenth century, see: H. Temple Patterson, *Poetic Genesis: Sébastien Mercier into Victor Hugo,* Vol. XI of *Studies on Voltaire and the Eighteenth Century,* ed. Theodore Besterman (Les Délices, Geneva: Institut et Musée Voltaire, 1960).

13. John Locke, *The Philosophical Works,* ed. J. A. St. John (London: George Bell and Sons, 1908), I, 227.

14. John Locke, *Essai philosophique concernant l'entendement humain où l'on montre quelle est l'étendue de nos connoissances certaines, et la manière dont nous y parvenons,* trans. Pierre Coste, 4th ed. (Amsterdam: Pierre Mortier, 1750), I, 223.

15. *Ibid.,* p. ix.

16. Denis Diderot, *Lettres sur les aveugles à l'usage de ceux qui voient,* in *Oeuvres complètes de Diderot,* ed. J. Assézat and M. Tourneux (Paris: Garnier, 1875), I, 294.

17. "Quasimodo" is found in the words of the Introit of the Mass for the first Sunday after Easter: *Quasimodo geniti infantes. . . .* The following works have notes about the name, "Quasimodo": Victor Hugo, *Notre-Dame de Paris,* ed. Larguier and Digeon (Paris: Bordas, 1949), I, 275; 276. Victor Hugo, *Notre-Dame de Paris: 1482,* ed. Marius-François Guyard (Paris: Garnier, 1961), p. 176. Victor Hugo, "Reliquat de Notre-Dame de Paris," in *Oeuvres complètes,* ed. Ollendorff (Paris: L'Imprimérie Nationale, 1904), Roman II, 427-433.

These references list various names which Hugo at one time or other had considered for his character: Malenfant, Mardi-Gras, Babylas, Quatre-Vents, Guerf, Mammès, Ovide, and Ischirion.

18. Victor Hugo, "Notes de l'édition," in *Oeuvres complètes,* ed. Ollendorff (Paris: L'Imprimérie Nationale, 1904), Roman II, 445.

19. Joseph Sauveur, *Principes d'acoustique et de musique, ou système général des intervalles des sons, et de son application à tous les systèmes et à tous les instrumens de musique,* inserted in *Mémoires de l'Académie Royale des Sciences* for 1701, pp. 1-68. Sauveur explained his purpose on page 1: "J'ai donc crû qu'il y avoit une science superieure à la Musique, que j'ay appellée *Acoustique,* qui a pour objet le Son en general, au lieu que la Musique a pour objet le Son entant qu'il est agreable à l'oüie." Accents follow the original.

See also: *Application des sons harmoniques à la composition des jeux d'orgues,* inserted in *Mémoires de l'Académie Royale des Sciences* for 1702, pp. 1-23.

20. Venzac, *Les Premiers Maîtres de Victor Hugo,* p. 302. The university listing was: "Applications de l'algèbre à la géométrie ou sections coniques —d'après Le Traité de Mr Lacroix, ou celui des courbes du second degré de Mr Biot.*

Two publications by Biot are: *Essai sur l'histoire générale des sciences pendant la révolution française* (Paris: Duprat et Fuchs, An XI [1803]); *Traité élémentaire d'astronomie physique* (Paris: Bernard, An XIII [1805]), 2 vols.

21. French plays dealing with deafness and muteness from the Middle Ages to the present have been listed and summarized by René Bernard in *Surdité, surdi-mutité et mutisme dans le théâtre français* (Paris: L. Rodstein, 1941). This study lists 160 plays having in the title the words, "deaf" and "mute." In addition, the titles of some 400 French plays having a plot revolving around deafness, deaf-muteness, or muteness are listed.

22. Victor Hugo, *Correspondance* (Paris: Calmann-Lévy, 1896), I, 150.

23. Maine de Biran, *Influence de l'habitude sur la faculté de penser,* p. 27.

24. Bernard, *Surdité, surdi-mutité et mutisme dans le théâtre français,* pp. 110-111.

# CHAPTER III

1. William Faulkner, "The Bear," in *The Faulkner Reader* (New York: Random House, 1953), p. 266. All citations from "The Bear," "That Evening Sun," *The Sound and the Fury,* and the speech of acceptance of the Nobel Prize for Literature are to *The Faulkner Reader.* Page numbers are given in the text.

2. René Cruchet, *Le Syndrome hystérique* (Paris: J.-B. Baillière, 1951), p. 63. Cruchet concludes: "Concluons plus modestement que: subconscience, inconscience, aboulie, rétrécissement du champ de la conscience, séparation de conscience, dédoublement de la personnalité, automatisme psychologique, refoulement des états de conscience, dissolution et reconstruction, désagrégation des états de conscience, personnalité instinctive et personnalité corticale ou consciente, moi instinctif et moi rationnel ou noétique, etc., etc. . . . ne sont que des mots dont la richesse, encore augmentée par la terminologie freudienne, ne fait qu'habiller plus ou

moins harmonieusement un processus mental qui, convenons-en, nous échappe encore à peu près complètement." Dr. Pierre Janet also wrote of the difficulty of defining the word, "hysteria." See: Pierre Janet, *L'Etat mental des hystériques,* 2nd ed. (Paris: Alcan, 1911), p. 412, p. 447.

3. Pierre Janet, *L'Etat mental des hystériques,* 2nd ed. (Paris: Alcan, 1911), p. 6.
4. William Faulkner, *Faulkner in the University,* ed. Frederick L. Gwynn and Joseph L. Blotner (Charlottesville, Virginia: University of Virginia Press, 1959), p. 268.
5. *Ibid.,* p. 65.
6. Sigmund Freud, *Collected Papers,* trans. Joan Rivière (London: Hogarth Press, 1948), I, 29.
7. Sigmund Freud, *The Basic Writings,* ed. and trans. A. A. Brill (New York: Random House, 1938), p. 457.
8. Janet, *L'État mental des hystériques,* p. 325.
9. Freud, *The Basic Writings,* p .512. See also Janet, *L'État mental des hystériques,* p. 336 and pp. 415-421. Janet wrote: "La combinaison la plus simple se rencontre lorsque deux attaques de nature différente, causée l'une de l'autre par des phénomènes psychologiques différentes et indépendantes, se juxtaposent, se succèdent et semblent constituer une même crise."
10. Freud, *Collected Papers,* II, 100.
11. Pierre Briquet, *Traité clinique et thérapeutique de l'hystérie* (Paris: J.-B. Baillière, 1859), pp. 600-601.
12. Faulkner, *Faulkner in the University,* p. 1. See also pages 6, 17, 31, and 32. Among other references to Caddy's role are: *Faulkner at Nagano,* ed. Robert A. Jelliffe (Tokyo: The Kenkyusha Press, 1956), pp. 103-105; *The Faulkner-Cowley File,* ed. Malcolm Cowley (New York: The Viking Press, 1966), p. 38.
13. William Faulkner, *Faulkner at Nagano,* ed. Robert A. Jelliffe (Tokyo: The Kenkyusha Press, 1956), p. 104. Faulkner's "stricken him blind at birth" recalls Gide's Gertrude in *La Symphonie pastorale* (1919).
14. William Faulkner, *Faulkner at West Point,* ed. Joseph L. Fant, III and Robert Ashley (New York: Random House, 1964), p. 116.
15. For a very different interpretation of Benjy, see: Winthrop Tilley, "The Idiot Boy in Mississippi," *American Journal of Mental Deficiency,* LIX (January 1955), 374-377.

## CHAPTER IV

1. Samuel Beckett, *Waiting for Godot* (New York: Grove Press, 1954), p. 6. Page numbers for other references to *Waiting for Godot* appear in the text.
2. Fyodor Dostoyevsky, *The Brothers Karamazov,* trans. Constance Garnett (New York: Random House, 1950), pp. 673-674.
3. André Gide, *Dostoïevski* (Paris: Gallimard, 1964), p. 207. I have translated the French into English.
4. Samuel Beckett, "Dante . . . Bruno . Vico . . Joyce," in *Our Exagmination Round His Factification for Incamination of Work in Progress* (New York: New Directions, 1961), p. 22.

5. The following works were followed for definitions of slang and thieves' words: Eric Partridge, *A Dictionary of Slang and Unconventional English* (New York: Macmillan, 1950); John S. Farmer and W. E. Henley, *Slang and Its Analogues: Past and Present* (Printed for Subscription Only: 1890-1891), 2 vols.

6. Henri Sauval, *Histoire et recherches des antiquités de la ville de Paris* (Paris: Moette et Chardon, 1724), I, 513.

7. Samuel Beckett, *Endgame* (New York: Grove Press, 1958), p. 57.

8. Paul Valéry, *Mauvaises pensées* (Paris: Gallimard, 1942), p. 95. I have translated the French into English.

9. Samuel Beckett, *Proust* (New York: Grove Press, 1951), p. 7.

10. Henri Bergson, *Le Rire*, 143rd ed. (Paris: Presses Universitaires de France, 1961), p. 29. I have translated the French into English.

11. Beckett, *Proust,* pp. 7-8.

12. *Ibid.,* p. 20.

# CHAPTER V

1. Among books which treat dwarfs and various abnormal characters in literature and art are: J.-M. Charcot and Paul Richer, *Les Difformes et les malades dans l'art* (Paris: Lecrosnier et Babé, 1889); Henry Meige, *Les Nains et les bossus dans l'art* (Paris: Lourdot, 1896); H. Bruchon, *Des Difformités, infirmités et maladies reproduites dans les oeuvres d'art* (Besançon: Dodivers, 1900).

2. Günter Grass, *Cat and Mouse,* trans. Ralph Manheim (New York: Harcourt, Brace and World, 1963), p. 22. Originally published in Germany under the title of *Katz und Maus,* 1961.

3. *Ibid.,* p. 118.

4. *Ibid.,* p. 134.

5. Günter Grass, *Dog Years,* trans. Ralph Manheim (New York: Harcourt, Brace and World, 1965). Originally published in Germany under the title, *Hundejahre,* 1963.

6. Günter Grass, *The Tin Drum,* trans. Ralph Manheim (New York: Pantheon Books, 1961), p. 60. Originally published in Germany under the title of *Die Blechtrommel,* 1959. All subsequent references to Oskar will be from *The Tin Drum* and page numbers will be given in the text.

7. For novels about cunning simpletons swindling their way through the war see: *The Good Soldier Schweik* by the Czech writer Jaroslav Hašek, translated into German in 1926, and Oskar Maria Graf's *Wir sind Gefangene,* 1928.

8. Marcel Proust spoke of "the immense edifice of memory" in *Du Côté de chez Swann.* He wanted to find lost time and asked whether past instants could be brought up to the surface of consciousness. Yes, by sensations, answered Proust in *Le Temps retrouvé:* "An hour is not only an hour, it is a vase filled with perfumes, sounds, projects, and climates. What we call reality is a certain connection between those sensations and those memories which surround us simultaneously. . . ."

9. Martin Heidegger, *Existence and Being,* 2nd ed. (London: Vision Press, 1956), p. 377.

10. In the poem, "Neue Mystik," published in 1967, Grass uses Hegel as an example of the temporary nature of each "ultimate" philosophy:

> While sceptics still stood aloof,
> nationalized tables were turned,
> spirits invoked, then fed
> on Hegel and other mystics,
> until there were knocks and legible answers.

The stanza is quoted from Günter Grass, *New Poems,* trans. Michael Hamburger (New York: Harcourt, Brace and World, 1968), p. 59.

11. Günter Grass, "Discours de remerciement," *Les Lettres Nouvelles,* décembre 1965-janvier 1966, p. 316. Another article about the writer and politics is: Ernst Wendt, "Zur Person und zur Sache: Günter Grass über Politik und Poesie," *Theater Heute,* April 1967, pp. 6-10.

# CHAPTER VI

1. Alain Robbe-Grillet, *Pour un nouveau roman* (Paris: Les Éditions de Minuit, 1963), p. 73.